RELIGIONS OF THE WORLD

I Am Hindu

✤ DEVI S. AIYENGAR ✤

The Rosen Publishing Group's
PowerKids Press™
New York

Published in 1996 by The Rosen Publishing Group, Inc.
29 East 21st Street, New York, NY 10010

First Edition

Book design: Erin McKenna and Kim Sonsky

Photo credits: Cover by Guillermina DeFerrari; pp. 4, 20 © Renato Rotolo/Gamma Liaison; p. 7 © C. Arvind/Gamma Liaison International; p. 8 © SEF/Art Resource, NY; p. 11 © Borromeo/Art Resource, NY; pp. 12, 16 © Bridgeman/Art Resource, NY; p. 15 © Art Resource, NY; p. 19 © P. Dewilde/Gamma Liaison.

Aiyengar, Devi S.
   I am Hindu / by Devi S. Aiyengar.
      p.   cm. — (Religions of the world)
   Includes index.
   Summary: A child introduces the reader to the Hindu religion.
   ISBN 0-8239-2381-9
   1. Hinduism—Juvenile literature. [Hinduism.] I. Title. II. Series: Religions of the world (Rosen Publishing Group).
BL1203.A49 1996
294.5—dc20   96-6992
                                                                                                                    CIP
                                                                                                                    AC

Manufactured in the United States of America

Contents

Being Hindu

My name is Anil. I live in Houston. I am Hindu. The Hindu religion is very old. It began in India.

My parents are from India. India is a large country with many different kinds of people. There are many ways of practicing the Hindu religion. People in different parts of India **worship** (WER-ship) different gods in many ways.

◀ *The Hindu religion is practiced by people all over the world.*

Temples

Temples (TEM-pulz) are very important in our religion. Temples are where the gods and goddesses live, and where we worship and pray. We gather at temples to study, talk, and celebrate Hindu holidays. Often there is dancing and singing. My brother was married in our temple. My family and everyone in the community helped to build our temple.

Many Hindu people join together to build, paint, and maintain their temples. This temple is in India. ▶

Diwali

Each fall we celebrate **Diwali** (dee-WAH-lee). Diwali is a special day. It is our festival of lights. We light lamps in honor of the Goddess Lakshmi and to invite her to stay with our family. We ask her to give us the things we need for a comfortable life, such as money and good fortune. We cook and eat sweets made from milk. My mother says that in India, they set off firecrackers and have great festivals in the streets during Diwali.

◄ *This statue of the Goddess Lakshmi is in the Museum of Hanging Gardens in Bombay, India.*

9

Krishna's Birthday

Vishnu was a god who came to earth in many different forms. One time he was human, and his name was Krishna. Hindus celebrate the night that Krishna was born on earth. On that night, a wicked prince knew that Krishna was coming. He put Krishna's parents in prison, hoping to catch Krishna when he was born. But Krishna magically escaped.

Vishnu is an important god in the Hindu religion. ▶

Dussehra

On the holiday **Dussehra** (dus-SEH-rah) we celebrate the brave acts of Rama. Rama was a human prince who was another form of the god Vishnu. During Dussehra we put on a play. We dress up as different characters and act out how Rama destroyed the evil demon-king Ravana. Later we burn a statue of the demon king in a big fire. Our teachers at the temple say that this celebrates the victory of good over evil.

◄ *The Hindu believe that Rama was another form of Vishnu who came to live on earth.*

Ganesh

One of the most important Hindu gods is Ganesh. He has the head of an elephant and the body of a man. He always carries a bowl of sweets, which he loves to eat. He rides on the back of a rat. The rat is a fast, clever animal. It is a symbol of being able to get around problems.

My mother says that because we honor Ganesh, he will help us to resolve problems and be successful in life. He brings us good fortune and helps us avoid disasters.

The Hindu think of Ganesh as a guardian. ▶
They believe that he brings people good luck.

Marriage

When my brother, Ashok, was ready to ask Poona to marry him, my parents met with Poona's parents to make sure they agreed to the wedding. They did.

When Ashok and Poona were married, Poona wore a bright, red **sari** (SAH-ree). Ashok wore a suit and a turban. During the ceremony, the priest tied Ashok's turban to Poona's sari. Then they walked around a sacred fire seven times together. This was to show that they were joined together as one.

◀ *A red sari is the traditional dress for a Hindu bride. This painting shows the Hindu god Rama and his brothers getting married.*

17

India

Next summer, my family and I are going on a journey to the **sacred** (SAY-kred) places in India. We will visit the **Himalayas** (him-al-LAY-ahz), which are mountains. The **Ganges River** (GAN-jeez RIV-ur) starts in the Himalayas. Hindus believe that the Ganges River is one of the most sacred places in the world. We believe that the river is a goddess, Ganga. Sometimes people throw flowers into the river to honor her.

Some Hindu go into the Ganges River to receive the blessing of Ganga. ▶

The Bhagavad Gita

My father says that there are many holy writings in our religion. One of them is the **Bhagavad Gita** (BA-ga-vad GHEE-ta). Many Hindus read the Bhagavad Gita. It tells the story of how Krishna was born on earth to teach Arjuna. Arjuna was a warrior. Arjuna had a difficult time during one very important battle. Krishna taught Arjuna about doing the right thing without letting his own needs, wants, or fears get in the way. Krishna teaches us to do the same thing through the Bhagavad Gita.

◀ *The temple is a place where many Hindu pray and read the Bhagavad Gita.*

Home Shrine

We have a special room in our house where we pray and worship. My mother and I light lamps every morning and burn **incense** (IN-sents). First we wash ourselves. We must be pure and clean to do our worship. Then my mother lets me ring the bell that tells the gods and goddesses that we wish to pray. I also arrange the tray of food we offer to them. Then we sing a hymn together before we leave to start our day.

Glossary

Bhagavad Gita (BA-ga-vad GHEE-ta) A holy book.

Diwali (dee-WAH-lee) Festival celebrating the Goddess Lakshmi; also called the Hindu festival of lights.

Dussehra (dus-SEH-rah) Celebration honoring Rama, a human representation of the god Vishnu.

Ganges River (GAN-jeez RIV-ur) Sacred river.

Himalayas (him-al-LAY-ahz) Mountains in India.

incense (IN-sents) Spice that is burned.

sacred (SAY-kred) Holy.

sari (SAH-ree) Traditional Indian dress for a girl or woman.

temples (TEM-pulz) Places of worship.

worship (WER-ship) Praise and respect shown for a god or goddess.

Index